The Islamic System of Government

Grand Ayatollah Muhammad Shirazi

fountain books

BM Box 8545
London WC1N 3XX
UK

In association with
Al-Kawthar Fountain Books
PO Box 11851
Dasmah 35159
Kuwait

First published 2000.

© *fountain books*

ISBN 1-903323-01-0

Table of Contents

Translator's Foreword

One of the laws of nature is the law of gravity. Given the law of gravity, no one may operate successfully an aircraft, say, if it has been designed in defiance of this law. Mankind therefore does his utmost to understand the laws of nature in order to use those laws to his advantage. Every single scientific discovery is a process of understanding one of the laws of nature. Every application of a discovery is based on one or more of these laws. If the design of that particular system contains the slightest deviation from the laws of nature, then its performance will be less than perfect, if not a total failure. In order to secure his success and progress, therefore, mankind always ensures to comply with the laws of nature - designed by Allah, the creator of all existence, whether or not he recognises them as being the laws of Allah.[1]

Just as mankind is obliged to accept the Earth's gravity and comply with its effects, he also needs to recognise the existence of other laws which affect him in other areas of life and the need to implement them in his life to ensure success and progress in every area. If the "disobedience" of the physical laws of nature results in immediate, and perhaps unpleasant consequences, the same may not be said for the laws of nature in other domains, and when the results or the consequences of a "disobedience" are realised, things might then be a little too late.

It is important therefore to recognise the existence and the need for laws, which govern mankind in the personal, social, economical, spiritual, etc. domains as well as in the physical domains.

Some might deny the existence, need or relevance of such laws which affect mankind in various domains. This is reminiscent of those who refused to accept that the Earth rotates round the sun, but their refusal did not mean that the solar system did not exist as we know it.

---

[1] *"Do they seek for other than the law of Allah? While all creatures in the heavens and on earth have, willing or unwilling, bowed to His Will, and to Him shall they all be brought back."* The Holy Qur'an, The House of Imran (3): 83.

Some of these laws may be discovered by man after years or even centuries of experimentation or trial and error. On the other hand he may use the guidance of his creator to his advantage in the quest for his perfection. Such laws are identified by mankind's creator and conveyed to mankind through His messengers. Having received these laws from the Holy Qur'an and the Teaching of the prophet, mankind is then able to conform to and implement these laws to fashion a kind of life he envisages himself living.

This publication outlines the basic structure of a system of government which, based on the laws of Allah, provides the ideal solution to mankind.

When it was suggested that one of the books of the author be translated into English, the question raised was what is the aim of this task. The aim of this translation is to try to show the true picture of the teachings of Islam to the English reader.

In the mass media and the subsequent stereotyping, Islam has been portrayed as a religion and/or an institution of violence, aggression or suppression. Islam has even been presented as the enemy and the source of threat and intimidation.

The aim of this work is to outline that Islam is a source of mercy and compassion to mankind and a school of guidance for human society.

It is to give a brief but accurate account of Islam and its teachings that this work aims for. It should provide enough insight into Islam to enable the reader even to challenge those who claim to adhere to Islam and yet commit actions in contradiction to the teachings of Islam and its values. Violence and atrocities committed in the name of the religion have no place in Islam and in fact the author is well known for his views on non-violence as a basic Islamic principle.

Throughout the history of human civilisation, the system of government has been an important issue and various schools, old and new, such as those of the ancient Romans and the regimes found today such as Marxist, Socialist and Capitalist have evolved in the course of time.

Islam is a complete system of life and it therefore sets out a system of government, which encompasses all the concerns of man and his society in harmony with his nature. Within this system, it gives the solutions to the different problems mankind faces at the present time under the various systems of governments including those in the Islamic countries. It was for such a reason that this book was translated to enable the reader to access some of the truth about the teachings of Islam.

Not only amongst the non-Muslims, but there are many Muslims who assume that Islam has nothing to do with life and such matters as politics, economics, sociology, etc. The systems of Islam have been distorted in minds of such individuals, and therefore they are unaware of the nature of Islamic government and the constituents of Islamic countries. They cannot differentiate between the Islamic way of life and life in its current form. The majority of Muslims might consider that only gambling and alcoholic drinks are forbidden and that only the daily prayers, fasting (during the month of Ramadahn) and going to pilgrimage (in Makkah) are mandatory. Such individuals therefore regard Muslim scholars as those who have no concern other than religious doctrine and worship. This publication: "The Islamic System of Government" gives a brief outline of some of the laws of Islam.

The author is of one of the most prominent scholars and religious authorities in the Muslim world. Ayatollah Muhammad Shirazi has written various specialised studies that are considered to be among the most important references in the Islamic sciences of beliefs, ethics, politics, economics, sociology, law, human rights, etc. He has enriched the world with his staggering contribution of some 980 books, treatise and studies on various branches of learning. His works range from simple introductory books for the young generations to literary and scientific masterpieces. Deeply rooted in the holy Qur'an and the Teachings of the Prophet of Islam, his vision and theories cover areas such as Politics, Economics, Government, Management, Sociology, Theology, Philosophy, History and Islamic Law. His work on Islamic Jurisprudence (al-Fiqh series) for example constitutes 150 volumes, which run into more than 67,000 pages.

This book consists of 15 sections and a conclusion. Each section covers a particular topic such as aim of government, foreign policy, political parties, government income, education, health, wealth, crime, freedom, judiciary and limits of government power. Various issues of each of the above topics are outlined in the form of articles.

The statements made in this book reflect the basic and fundamental nature of the right or issue involved in each case.

One of the issues, which are of particular interest to the author, is freedom. The fundamental principle in mankind is freedom, the author states. If, in the interest of other higher priority(s), in the short term or under exceptional circumstances, some of those rights may not be exercised, then as a last resort, some restrictions may be imposed. The imposition of such restrictions is not only short term, but more importantly it is also to help to strive to reach a state where those restrictions become redundant and therefore lifted altogether.

This book presents the Islamic system which, unfortunately, has not been implemented anywhere in the world.

The views of the author on these topics are detailed in a number of his books, some of which have been referred to in the course of this translation:

- *al-Fiqh* series, volumes 105-106: Politics
- *al-Fiqh* series, volumes 107-108: Economics
- *al-Fiqh* series, volumes 109-110: Sociology
- *al-Fiqh* series, volumes 101-102: Islamic Government
- *al-Fiqh* series, volume 100: Rights
- *al-Fiqh* series, volume 139: Law
- *al-Fiqh* series, volumes 103-104: Management
- The New Order for the World of Faith, Freedom, Prosperity and Peace
- The Process of Change
- Contemporary Islamic Economic System

It should be noted that:

The sections of Glossary, References and Bibliographies located at the end of the book are included by the translator.

The *italic* Arabic words and relevant terms are explained in the glossary.

The words in brackets ( ) are added by the translator for clarification.

In almost all cases, the footnotes are those of the translator.

Z. Olyabek

July 1998

In the name of Allah, Most Compassionate, Most Merciful

Praise is to Allah, the Cherisher and Sustainer of the worlds and the Blessings and Peace be upon he who has been sent as Mercy to the worlds; Muhammad and his purified posterity.

Chapter 1: General Principles

Article 1

Islam[2] is a complete system of life, devised by a wise and just deity, for the good and prosperity of mankind, both in this world and hereafter. Any system that defies the Islamic system is therefore inadequate and does not provide the best for mankind.

Article 2

Allah defines the laws of Islam[3], and mankind may not make a law in contradiction to laws of Allah[4]. Some of these laws are outlined in the Glorious Qur'an. The prophet Muhammad, through his Teaching (the *Sunnah*), explained and expanded these Islamic laws[5]. The

---

[2] Islam is derived from the Arabic word for peace and it is harmony to the laws of Allah and the teachings of Islam are based on the nature of mankind. Islam is a set of teachings that has been revealed by Allah to mankind. The revelation of Islam has taken place, at various times, through the different messengers of Allah such as Noah, Abraham, Moses, Jesus and finally Muhammad peace be upon them.

[3] Allah is the Arabic name (Eloha in Hebrew) for the only creator of all existence.

[4] The principles and laws defined by Allah are more reliable than those made by man for three main reasons:
- Allah, the creator of the worlds and all existence, has complete knowledge of the nature of mankind and all existence in the universe, and therefore knows the 'good' laws from the 'bad' laws. On the other hand, mankind does not have total command and understanding of his nature and that of the universe.
- Allah is not affected by desires and temptations, and therefore His laws are set to the best interest of mankind, whereas mankind, however self-disciplined he may be, is affected by instincts, temptations, social pressures, etc. and this leads to laws which are not in his best interest.

Man-made laws are not respected as the executor is man and thus crime and corruption is on the increase. However Divine laws are whole-heartedly respected and therefore in societies governed by Allah's laws, crime is very low if not extinct. From M. Shirazi, "al-Fiqh series", 150 vols., vol. 106, "Politics", pp 289-299.

[5] The Prophet's Teachings are also based on revelations from Allah.

1

prophet also delegated the explanations of some of the laws to his successors; the infallible *Imams*[6]. They in turn explained and clarified the laws of Islam, precisely according to the Qur'an and the Teaching of the prophet.

Article 3

Islamic laws rely on two main sources:

1. The Glorious Qur'an.

2. The Teaching of the prophet Muhammad peace be upon him (PBUH).

The latter are a combination of the "words", "deeds" and "endorsements" of the holy prophet and - by extension - those of the rest of the 14 infallible individuals[7].

There are two other sources that are secondary to the above two:

3. Consensus of the learned religious scholars. This only becomes a "source" if it leads to the Teaching of the prophet or, by extension, the infallible Imams.

4. Reason, the framework of which is indicated by the Teaching (of the prophet).[8]

Article 4

According to the Glorious Qur'an and the Teaching of the Prophet, the laws are categorised in two groups:

Specific laws: Such as the mandate of the daily prayers or the illegality of adultery. Such laws may never be changed.

General laws: Such laws define the basic principles and are applied to various cases and new developments.

---

[6] There are 12 infallible *Imams* (leaders) appointed by Allah through his messenger Muhammad (PBUH). This first of them being Ali and the last of them Mahdi, born in the ninth century, will emerge to establish peace and justice by Allah's Will.

[7] The 14 infallible individuals are the Prophet, his daughter Fatimah and the 12 Imams of his progeny, all of whom are also known as *"Ahl-ul-Bayt"*.

[8] Reason, on the other hand, forms the basis of Islamic legislation and its sources.

For example: *"Any intoxicant is prohibited"*,

"Everything is permissible (Halaal) unless it is stated to be prohibited (Haraam).

Such laws are flexible and may be applied at any time and place. Using the above example, therefore, any intoxicant which did not exist at the time of the prophet and hence there has been no ruling from the prophet about it, is still subjected to the above law. Similarly, any new food or medical product, which does not contain banned materials, is permissible.

Article 5

Any aspect, old or new, specific or general is subjected to an Islamic law. There is not a single issue or question that Islam has remained silent about or has not identified a ruling for.

According to Islamic Jurisprudence, laws may be classified into two main categories: the *"Statutory"* laws and the *"Instituted"* laws.

The *"Statutory"* laws are divided into five categories:

Mandatory:	An obligatory act - one must do.
Prohibition:	A forbidden or illegal act - one must abstain from committing such action.
Desirable:	A desirable but not obligatory act - one is encouraged to do.
Undesirable:	An undesirable but not forbidden act - one is discouraged to do.
Permissible:	Any act which is neither mandatory nor prohibited and one is therefore free to do or not do.

The *"Instituted"* laws are those which are outside the bounds of *"Statutory"* laws.[9]

---

[9] For example Contracts, Agreements or Understanding on specific issues between individuals concerned; such as marriage are governed by the *"Instituted"* laws. Details in jurisprudence texts.

Article 6

It is imperative for any Muslim to act according to the Islamic laws in all aspects of (her/his) life. To do this (s) he must either:

- gain sufficient knowledge of Islamic laws e.g. by going to university etc. in order to understand and derive the laws as required, i.e. become an expert (known as *Mujtahid*) in this field; or

- seek the guidance of a qualified learned scholar known as *Marje'* [10] or 'mentor'. In the latter case one may refer all their enquiries to their *Marje'*.

Those who have some background in Jurisprudence may opt to choose from those rulings expressed by a *Marje'* in order to be on the safe side.

Chapter 2: System of Government

Article 7

As mentioned earlier, legislation is for Allah only and that no one, whatever their status, may establish a law in contradiction to that of Islam. Mankind may attempt to understand the laws of Allah and derive them from the Book (of Allah, i.e. the Glorious Qur'an) and the Teaching (of the prophet Muhammad, known as the *Sunnah*). We may refer to this understanding and derivation as 'legislation' and 'law making'.

Article 8

The leader or the Head of State under the Islamic system of government is the *Mujtahid* [11] who satisfies all the criteria required, (in the case of there being a single *Mujtahid*.) If there were more than one *Mujtahid*, the Head of State is the leadership 'council of scholars' which consists of the *Mujtahids*. Under the consultative leadership system, the public elects the *Mujtahid* council members.

---

[10] A *Marje'* is necessarily a *Mujtahid*.

[11] A *Mujtahid* is a learned scholar in the Islamic sciences such as Jurisprudence, Qur'an, Teaching of the prophet, Logic, etc. who is accordingly competent to derive the rulings required for any case.

The Criteria for the *Mujtahid* are:

Ijtihaad: Which is the knowledge, expertise and ability to derive the ruling required for any case using the four sources of reference, i.e. the Qur'an, the Teaching of the Prophet (*Sunnah*), Unanimity and Reason.[12]

Justice: To have a state of self-discipline that enables him to abstain from committing any major illicit act (sin) or persisting on minor ones.

Male Gender: It is not appropriate for a woman to hold this position.[13]

Freedom: The Head of State must have his own free will.[14]

Legitimate Birth: As an individual of illegitimate birth is not suited for such a post.

There are also other criteria such as 'Adolescence', 'Sound Mind', 'Faith', etc. that do not require further comments.

Article 9

---

[12] As mentioned in Article 3.

[13] This is to avoid the female from being subjected to the pressures of the tasks involved. This is purely on biological / physiological grounds and it is not a question of capability nor does it reflect any lesser value being attributed to women, since the male and female individuals are treated on the basis of their faith and deed and no other criterion, as stated in the Qur'an: *"O mankind! We created you from a single (pair) of a male and a female, and made you into nations and tribes, that you may know each other (not that you may despise each other). Verily the most honoured of you in the sight of Allah is the most righteous of you. And Allah has full Knowledge and is well acquainted (with all things)."*, The Qur'an, Apartments (50): 13. Latest scientific research programs have shown that they (men and women) have significant differences in the brain structure, enabling them for differing tasks. For detailed discussions see A. Moir and B. Moir, "Why Men Don't Iron", HarperCollins Publishers, 1998. See also M. Shirazi, "al-Fiqh series", 150 vols., vol. 106, "Politics", pp 282-286, M. Shirazi, "al-Fiqh series", 150 vols., vol. 102, "Islamic Government", pp 97-123, and M. Shirazi, "The New Order for the World of Faith, Freedom, Prosperity and Peace", pp 49-52.

[14] The *Mujtahid* must be free from and independent of any pressure from other individual, group, organisation, government etc.

5

The powers[15] are independent form each other.

These powers may only be "in the hands" of the Head of State if the majority of the public agrees to this and provided that such measures are taken as to ensure that there is no likelihood of this eventually leading to an dictatorship system.

It is of utmost importance to establish a system of party-political pluralism in the country.

Article 10

1. If there was only one *Mujtahid* who meets all the required criteria then he is automatically the Head of State.

2. If there were more than one, the *Mujtahids* elected by the public elect one *Mujtahid* or group of them to lead the country.

3. The nation may instead, opt to elect the leader of the country or the leadership council directly.

Article 11

The term of office of the Head of State terminates if he loses 'credibility', i.e. if he no longer meets one of the conditions of the criteria, or if he dies.

The nation may replace the Head of State and it may decide the duration of the term of office of the leader as well as the number of terms he may serve.

Monarchy or leadership through inheritance is not accepted in Islam and despotism is rejected. Also the Head of State may not remain in power without the approval of the nation.

Article 12

The elected Head of State may appoint the Head of Government e.g. Prime Minister. The head of government should be a trustworthy, competent and knowledgeable in Islamic law but does not have to be a *Mujtahid*. The two heads must co-operate in the process of running the affairs of the country.

---

[15] These are the Judiciary, the Executive, the Legislative (see Article 7) and, in the opinion of the author, the Media is the 4th power.

Article 13

Criteria based on country, nationality, race, etc. are not required as pre-conditions for the Head of State and in fact such conditions are not accepted in Islam.

Article 14

If the Head of State should lose some of the criteria, Muslims must not follow him. It is imperative that measures are taken to redress this issue, and if the subsequent outcome proved satisfactory he may, with the approval of the nation, resume his term of office. In the event of an unsatisfactory outcome or that the loss was irreversible, e.g. if he become insane, he must be removed from office immediately.

Article 15

It is imperative for the Head of State to consult with others. In order to set a precedent, the prophet Muhammad used to consult with his selected companions on the affairs of state. Taking lead from the prophet's consultation policy, other Muslim rulers used to practise this policy too.

Article 16

No Muslim may raise arms against the elected Islamic authority or the state and if so, those involved should be returned back to the Muslim community.[16]

Article 17

Every country may have a Head of State with the aforementioned criteria, but the preferred option by far is that all the Muslim countries come under one Islamic government similar to some countries at the present time.

Chapter 3: The Aim of the Islamic Government
Article 18

The aim of an Islamic government is to:

---

[16] i.e. comply with the order of the community.

- implement Islam in all matters of government and society; to take the Muslims forward; and to bring about prosperity in the domains of economy, politics and all other areas.

- invite other nations to Islam,

- help and rescue the deprived and the oppressed in all nations from the oppressing forces.

Article 19

Implementation of Islam inside the country aims to:

- Create an ideal Muslim community with its distinct features and elements and safeguard its independence in the various domains: political, economics, cultural, etc.

- Provide Islamic Freedoms[17] in the various domains: manufacturing, agriculture, trade, press, media, etc. taking lead from the basic principles:

    "People are masters of their own wealth and lives"[18], and

    "Let there be no compulsion in religion, Truth stands out clear from Error.."[19]

- Reject any law which is in contradiction to Islam,

- Cleansing the society from decadence, crime and corruption,

- Eliminate illiteracy and ignorance,

- Fight against poverty and raising the standard of living,

- Eradicate disease and illness throughout the society through preventative means and provide nation-wide health service,

- Establish the institution of social justice,

- Unite the Muslim community under one banner and overcome divisions and discriminations in any form or shape,

---

[17] M. Shirazi, "The New Order for the World of Faith, Freedom, Prosperity and Peace", and
   M. Shirazi, "al-Fiqh series", 150 vols., vol. 138, "The Freedoms".

[18] M. B. Majlesi (ed.), "Seas of Lights", 110 vols., vol. 2, p 272.

[19] The holy Qur'an, The Cow (2): 256.

- Provide the country with the best defence system against outside aggression, *"Make ready your strength to the utmost of your power."*[20]

- Safeguard Islamic values and establish its laws in all corners of the land,

- Lead the society forward in all the domains and fundamentals of life,

- Provide the opportunity for all individuals, groups, organisations to compete in the above tasks;

> *"Be quick in the race for forgiveness from your Lord."*[21]

and

> *"Race each other towards all that is good."*[22]

Article 20

The government will implement Islam in the society and realise the aims mentioned above by the cleanest means and the purest methods with which honesty, truth, justice and fairness are associated.

The principle of "the end justifies the means" is not accepted in Islam.

Article 21

Article 20 is totally upheld in the government's foreign policy too. The Islamic government observes the truth, honesty and justice in its dealings with all other governments of the world.

Chapter 4: Foreign Policy

Article 22

The Islamic government adopts the policy of brotherhood in every aspect towards other Islamic governments. If an Islamic government

---

[20] The holy Qur'an, The Public Estate (8): 60.

[21] The holy Qur'an, The Family of Imran (3): 133.

[22] The holy Qur'an, The Table Spread (5): 48.

faces any harm or danger, all other Islamic governments must support and align themselves with the troubled government: *"the Muslims are as a single body."*[23]

The Islamic government must consider all other Islamic governments as itself since, despite their apparent variety, they are one in principle, aim and message.

Islam rejects any divisions, discriminations or favouritism.

Article 23

Any economical, cultural, military, . . . alliance, agreement or deal may not be entered into if such co-operation leads to any foreign control over Muslim country(s).

Article 24

The Islamic government adopts a policy of friendship, harmony and co-operation towards non-Muslim governments, which do not wage war against Islam; as stated in the Holy Qur'an:

> *"Allah forbids you not, with regard to those who fight you not for (your) Faith nor drive you out of your homes, from dealing kindly and justly with them: for Allah loves those who are just."*[24]

Article 25

Towards non-Muslim governments who do wage war against Islam, the Islamic government adopts the policy of peace as far as possible, otherwise that of war as a last resort. However war in Islam is an extremely clean one and unlike those we see in the world today[25].

---

[23] M. B. Majlesi (ed.), "Seas of Lights", 110 vols., vol. 61, p 148.

[24] The holy Qur'an, The Tested (60): 8.

[25] Islam is inherently based on peace and it does not resort to war unless it is absolutely necessary and when there is no other alternative; just as one only undergoes a medical operation when it is vital to do so. The last prophet of Islam, Muhammad peace be upon him, never engaged in any battle unless he was forced to do so. Even then, he never started a battle and always used to wait until his opponent attacked him. Furthermore, the prophet used to ensure the level of engagement was kept to an absolute minimum. He used to ask his companions to respect the defeated side and

Article 26

All international agreements may be entered into after consultation with the elected leadership council of religious authorities.

Chapter 5: Sects

Article 27

The various sects or groups, in an Islamic country, may be divided in three categories:

1. The Islamic sects;

2. The non-Islamic religious sects (*People of the Book*);

3. Other sects.

Regarding the Islamic sects, the government may not exert any pressure or intimidation on the followers of any of the sects. Every sect may practice their personal and religious affairs according to their own jurisprudence, and refer to their own scholars and judges.

The people of the book are the Jews, the Christians and the Zoroastrians. When living in an Islamic country they are referred to as *Ahl-ul-Thimmah*, where their safety and security are the responsibility of Islam. Their lives and wealth are protected and any transgression on their rights will be prosecuted according to Islamic laws. Under Islamic law these religious sects will be treated according to their own laws, on the basis of the principle:

> *"Enjoin on them whatever they have enjoined on themselves"*[26]

---

used to say: *"Amongst the best moral values in this world and thereafter is to forgive he who did harm to you, speak well to him and be generous to him when you have power over him."*

It is therefore a major duty of the Islamic government to do all it possibly can to put an end to "the arms race" and "military *coup d'état*" between which the world is trapped. As a result, wars and military *coup d'état* have become widespread and arms production and export have become the biggest money generators in the world. The end result is that humanity is trapped between the nightmare of war and that of poverty. From M. Shirazi, "al-Fiqh series", 150 vols., vol. 99, "The Rule of Islam", pp 133-136.

[26] M. H. al-Hur al-Ameli (ed.), "The Shi'a Guide to Islamic Law", vol. 17, p 485.

As for the third category, i.e. those who believe in religions other than those mentioned above or in no religion at all, it is for the Islamic government to try to guide them to and show them the truth and invite them to Islam, just as the prophet Muhammad (PBUH) treated the atheists and pagans of Makkah and other places.[27]

Chapter 6: Political Parties and Social Divisions

Article 28

As mentioned earlier (Article 2), legislation is for Allah only and therefore parliaments in Islam do not legislate (fundamental laws). The purpose of parliaments in Islam is to legislate within the framework of Islam; and this legislation is of the form of derivation of laws as stated in Article 7. "Upper" and "Lower" Houses of parliament may exist for the purpose of implementing Islam and managing the affairs of the country.

Article 29

(Political) parties in Islam are not intended to create the two houses of parliaments for the purpose of law making. Rather, through their organised activities, they are to re-establish the rule of Islam, provided they operate according to the jurisdiction of a religious authority and within the framework of Islamic laws.[28] The creation

---

[27] i.e. the pagans were at liberty to exercise their beliefs under the Islamic rule after Makkah's fall and the prophet's call to Islam. *"Let there be no compulsion in religion, Truth stands out clear from Error"* The holy Qur'an, The Cow (2): 256.
The author has shown that the *"Enjoin"* principle, above, is also applicable to the sects of the third category. See M. Shirazi, "al-Fiqh series", 150 vols., vol. 22, "Jurisprudence Fundamentals".

[28] Under secular systems the framework of political parties is the country, whereas the framework under the Islamic system is belief. In the so-called democratic countries, nationals from other countries are not allowed to form political parties and assume power in the country. Under the Islamic system, however, the framework is much wider than that of the secular system in that individuals are not judged by where they happened to be born or what "nationality papers" they carry but the only criteria is their faith. As opposed to only nationals of a particular country may assume power in that country, Muslims, of any country or nationality, may assume power under the Islamic system. From M. Shirazi, "al-Fiqh series", 150 vols., vol. 106, "Politics", pp 98-212.

of such parties becomes obligatory if there were no other means of re-establishing the rule of Islam.

Article 30

There is no discrimination in Islam on the basis of colour, language, sex, nationality, race, profession, etc. All Muslims are regarded as equal, belonging to a single community and believing in the message of Allah. However, Allah values them, according to their good deeds, virtue and piety.[29]

If a Muslim individual of one country travelled to or settled in another Muslim country, which had a different Head of State, then he would be equal to those resident of that country. He may not be discriminated against in any minor or major issue and enjoy all the rights exercised by them. This is because all the different Islamic countries are Muslim's home.

Chapter 7: Government's Income

Article 31

The Islamic government's sources of income are:

1. *Khums*:   Tax of 20% levied on untaxed, superfluous annual income[30].

2. *Zakat*:   Tax on nine items when over certain limit[31].

3. *Jizyah*:   Non-Muslim Tax[32].

---

[29] *"O mankind! We created you from a single (pair) of a male and a female, and made you into nations and tribes, that you may know each other (not that you may despise each other). Verily the most honoured of you in the sight of Allah is the most righteous of you. And Allah has full Knowledge and is well acquainted (with all things)."*, The Qur'an, The Private Apartments (49): 13.

[30] The taxed capital is not subjected to future *Khums* tax. Details in M. Shirazi, "al-Fiqh series", 150 vols., vol. 33, "Khums".

[31] These items are Wheat, Barley, Dates, Raisins, Gold, Silver, Camels, Cows, and Sheep. Details in M. Shirazi, "al-Fiqh series", 150 vols., vols. 29-32, "Zakat".

[32] This is the tax that is paid by the non-Muslims under the Islamic system. The non-Muslims do not pay either the *Khums* or the *Zakat* taxes. They are not obliged to join the armed forces to defend the Islamic State whereas the Muslims are. The defence of

4. *Khiraj*:   The income from letting a particular category of land.[33]

This is in addition to any business and trade activities the government may engage in - provided the extent of such activities do not deprive or damage the interest of the public - as defined in the Islamic jurisprudence.

Article 32

There is no tax in Islam other than the four mentioned above. The government or any other person may not obtain any money from an individual by force, since

"People are the masters of their own wealth".

The exception to this is that, in emergency cases, the government may seek permission from the Head of State or the leadership council to endorse the imposition of a particular levy (for a limited time). In such cases exceptional measures are taken as deemed necessary for the circumstances.

Article 33

The government has no right to confiscate the wealth of the individuals under any pretext. Also the government may not, under the pretext of land or agricultural reforms, take away land and farms from their owners as *"Possession is 9/10 [ths] of the law"*.

If it was proved that an individual has been usurped of anything, the judiciary must return it back to the owner and not anyone else.

Article 34

The government's income is held in the *"Bayt-el-Maal"* or the Central Bank and is spent in the interest of the Muslims. The money surplus to requirement should be returned to the public, as the Prophet and *Ameer-ul-Mu'mineen*, Ali (PBUH) used to do.[34]

---

the non-Muslims' lives, wealth, dignity etc. is the responsibility of the Islamic State. See M. Shirazi, "al-Fiqh series", 150 vols., vol. 108, "Economics"; pp 41-42.

[33] Details in M. Shirazi, "al-Fiqh series", 150 vols., vol. 108, "Economics".

[34] The author is emphasising that the money belongs to the public, and it must be returned back to the public in some way. Here the author is not specifying the mechanism of implementing this.

Chapter 8: Education

Article 35

Islam has made *"The seeking of knowledge (is) mandatory for every male and female Muslim."*[35] Therefore it is imperative for all to know the teachings of Islam.

Article 36

It is imperative that Muslims gain sufficient knowledge[36] regarding all and every aspects of their personal and social lives in the fields of science, medicine, technology etc.

Article 37

* The government must provide the Muslims a complete system of education from schools to universities, libraries to publishing houses etc. to enable them to access all the different branches of knowledge.

* The government must value highly the importance of universities as centres of knowledge and excellence and allocate them with considerable budgets to attract the best resources and expertise required. It must also ensure that students and lecturers engage in research and development in free environments.

* The government should ensure that every member of the community is free to establish such institutions.

* The government should ensure that the Islamic State is at the forefront of science and technology as far as other countries of the world are concerned.

Article 38

It is imperative that all schools and universities are free from all illicit acts and means of decadence in all their forms.

---

[35] M. B. Majlesi (ed.), "Seas of Lights", 110 vols., vol. 1, page 177.

[36] . . . to the extent that the need of the society for experts in any particular field is met. Beyond this, it is no longer obligatory and it becomes an optional duty for the Muslim.

Chapter 9: Welfare

Article 39

There is no room for poverty in Islam:

- Individuals who are unable to earn their living expenses must receive financial support, according to their esteem, from the government to cover all aspects of their lives including marriage etc. The government must also support those who want to start up a business but need financial support.

- Travellers or those who are away from their homes and do not have the means to return home must receive appropriate help to return home.

- The Islamic government must pay the debt of those who have not used their loan for illicit purposes and cannot pay it back.

- The Islamic government must also pay the debt of the deceased who have not left any form of wealth behind.

Chapter 10: Health

Article 40

Islam's fight against the various forms of diseases are based on measures such as:

- The Islamic government must prevent the illicit and forbidden practices as defined under Islamic law[37] as such acts are the causes of many physiological and psychological illnesses in the society. The Islamic government must also prevent practices which lead to environmental pollution provided that the measures taken are based on the principle of

  "No (one may) harm (anyone) nor (be) harmed (by anyone) in Islam."[38]

- The provision of health care, or the means for it, for the poor who cannot afford the cost of the service themselves.

---

[37] Illicit acts such as prostitution, production and sale of alcoholic drinks, gambling etc.

[38] M. H. T. al-Noori (ed.), "Extension for the Guide", vol. 13, p 308.

- The Islamic government must naturally establish hospitals, clinics, medical universities, etc. It must also allow the public to participate in such schemes and establish such institutions.

Chapter 11: Crime

Article 41

There are no purpose-built prisons in Islam, for there is no precedent in building prisons at the time of the Prophet or his appointed successors; with the exception of a reported case at the time of *Imam* Ali which was built during an emergency situation[39].

If, under compelling circumstances, a prison were to be built temporarily, it should be with consultation and authorisation of the Head of State or the leadership council.

During the Islamic era, those who were sentenced to imprisonment were given to a member of the public to detain, say, in a spare room in his house or in an empty house until the detention period expires.[40]

Article 42

With the exception of a few cases, no one is imprisoned under the Islamic system. The exceptions are a fraudster who does not pay back his debt; such an individual is imprisoned until he pays his debt. Or a kidnapper (is imprisoned) who abducts a person to be killed by a third party.[41]

Article 43

---

[39] *Imam* Ali could not implement the Islamic punishments, *Hadd*, in this situation because system in place was corrupt when he assumed the government office. The illegal and illicit practices that had been taking place in the Islamic state during the reign of his predecessor meant that such practices had been deeply rooted in the society. Under such circumstances he could not implement the *Hadd* and had to resort to other means of punishment such as imprisonment. Islamic punishment may only be exercised when a true Islamic system has been established.

[40] . . . this reflects the nature and the state of the society of the day . . .

[41] the killer will receive capital punishment. M. Shirazi, "al-Fiqh series", 150 vols., vol. 100, "The Rights", p 354.

Most of the punishments defined by man-made laws are not recognised by Islam. Under Islamic law, it is illegal to detain anyone even in his own home. Therefore under Islamic rule, few prisoners will be found throughout the country. Crimes that are committed today may be categorised into three groups:

1. crimes, which are the result of the environment.

2. crimes, which are described by man-made laws as crimes but in fact, they are not.

3. crimes that are the result of natural deviations in an individual, which occur even in the best of societies.

As Islam provides a good and ideal environment and it does not recognise the man-made laws, there will be no crime in its society other than those of the third category, which is of minimal proportion. Therefore it is only rare when an individual in an Islamic society faces punishment.

Article 44

In principle, Islam does not recognise the payment of 'fine' as a punishment scheme, except in special cases such as compensation for causing death by accident or other damages. If there were exceptional circumstances where the Islamic government was to introduce such schemes, it must be with the approval of the majority of the leadership council.

Article 45

The punishment as defined under Islamic law, *Hadd*, may not be suspended through the intercession of a respected individual, etc.

Article 46

Islam has defined a set of punishments for specific crimes in order to purify human society. These punishments may not be modified or reduced. Every one stands equal in front of the law, from the highest ranking official, the leader or the Head of State to ordinary members of the public.

Article 47

In non-Islamic environments where the Islamic government is not fully established or the Islamic political, economic, and other systems

are not instituted, the code of punishment defined by Islam, i.e. the *Hadd*, may not be exercised. The offender, however, should be punished as seen fit by the judge.

The indicator for an established Islamic system is not just the rhetoric slogans but the overwhelming majority of the Islamic system and laws in politics, economics, social affairs, contracts, trade, etc. must be practically implemented and exercised.

Article 48

The Head of State has the authority of amnesty if it is in the wider interest of the state. The precedent for such authority is when the Prophet gave amnesty to the people of *Makkah* and on occasions when individuals were to be punished. Similarly *Ameer-ul-Mu'mineen*[42], Ali gave amnesty to the people of Basra and to some of those who were to be punished.

The Head of State in consultation with other religious authorities identifies the interest of the state on the basis of the highest priority when there is a conflict of interest between carrying out a verdict and, say, avoiding a civil unrest.

Article 49

Punishment under Islamic law is categorised into two groups:

1. Those defined in the holy Qur'an and the Teaching of the prophet known as *"Hadd"*;

2. Those determined by the judge, known as *"Ta'zeer"*.

Chapter 12: Freedom

Article 50

Islam is a collection of freedoms as stated in the holy Qur'an:

"He releases them from their heavy burdens and from the yokes that are upon them."[43]

---

[42] *Ameer-ul-Mu'mineen* is the title the Prophet Muhammad, PBUH, exclusively granted to Ali, PBUH, which means Master of the Faithful.

[43] The Qur'an, The Heights (7): 157

Therefore anything, which is not prescribed by Islam as obligatory or illicit, one is free to engage in. No one may deny or suppress any of the freedoms since:

"People are masters of their own wealth and lives." [44]

Article 51

Under an Islamic system, every one is free to engage in any legal activity for wealth generation:

- Agriculture: *"The land belongs to Allah and to whoever develops it."* [45]

- Manufacturing,

- Trade: *"Let the people sustain one another."*

- Invention,

- Procurement of the permissible in the seas such as fishing, pearl fishery and farming, etc.

- Procurement of the permissible in the earth such as mineral ores, coals, oil, etc.

- Procurement of the permissible on the land such as woods and forestry, hunting, etc.

- Procurement of the permissible in the air such as hunting birds, etc.

- Procurement of pasture, water etc. In general, the public has the right to use the (public estate) *Anfaal* [46].

- Procurement of anything abandoned and not owned by anyone.

The above mentioned all come under the category of

"He Who has created for you all things that are on earth"[47].

---

[44] M. B. Majlesi (ed.), "Seas of Lights", 110 vols., vol. 2, p 272.

[45] M. Y. al-Koleyni (ed.), "al-Kafi", vol. 3, p279.

[46] *Anfaal* is defined as those items that are not owned by anyone, i.e. Public Estate.

[47] The holy Qur'an, The Cow (2): 29.

The right of procurement is on the basis that others are not harmed or deprived of the same right, as well as those of the future generations. Therefore an individual or a group may not procure, say, all the oil wells, or procure them for more than their right to the extent that others are deprived of this, or any other right.

Article 52

The government or any other authority has no right to deny anyone the right to procure any of the above mentioned, or the right to engage in other professions or income generating occupations. The exception to this are those means which are declared illicit by Islam such as usury, gambling, (production and sale of) alcohol, etc.

Also the government or any other authority has no right to levy any taxes or duties etc. on any procurement or business activity unless in emergency cases and to prevent the public's *"loss of rights"*.[48]

Article 53

The general principle in Islam is that no import or export duties may be levied. This is regarded as denial of freedom and individual rights.

If, in emergency circumstances, such levies were to be introduced, for example if the local industry were to be protected, then the Head of State or the leadership council, in consultation with the experts in the field must consider the following issues:

- the illicit nature of such levies,

- the principle *"the people are masters of their wealth and their lives"*,

- the principle *"He releases them from their heavy burdens and from the yokes that are upon them"*[49],

---

[48] If the government was faced with financial difficulties and was unable to run the affairs of the country adequately and to meet its targets and responsibilities in education, housing, unemployment benefit, etc. then it may announce a set of temporary measures required to enable it to meet its obligations. These measures are in the form of temporary taxation schemes prescribed with the permission of the leadership council and after consultation with the business and wealthy communities. The *"loss of rights"* refers to the difficulties, which the public would sustain if the government were not to meet its responsibilities.

- the trade deficit between the two countries,

- the different inflation rates in the two countries,

- the principle of *"No harm may reach either side"* for the people and governments of countries as well as the workers and businesses involved.

Article 54

In principle, activities such as trade, fishing, mining, etc. do not require any permission, preconditions, or any charges, duties etc. Everyone is free to engage in such activities and any law, which prevents such activities or denies these freedoms, is not recognised, and therefore rejected, by Islam. Anyone who suppresses such freedoms is an offender. Furthermore, everyone may establish large companies, airports, railways and other means of transport, power (energy) generation, etc. [50]

Article 55

Land is classified into three categories[51]:

1. Land owned legally (by individuals, groups, government, etc.) according to Islamic law,

2. Land which is commonly owned by all Muslims,

3. Other lands.

---

[49] The Qur'an, The Heights (7): 157.

[50] In Islam the fundamental right of mankind is freedom. Freedom is the most precious entity for mankind. One such freedom is to engage in any activity without hindrance from anyone or any authority. The public has the priority over the authority if there is a conflict of interest and freedom between those of the public and those of the authority. Minimal regulation may be imposed only if deemed necessary to ensure order and avoid chaos, provided it does not result in deprivation of the individuals rights. When at a later stage such regulation were no longer needed, then they must be lifted. If any regulations are imposed, however, no charges or duties may be incurred on those who want to engage in the activities. An individual must not pay to exercise his/her right!
M. Shirazi, "al-Fiqh series", vol. 108, "Economics", pp 212-213.

[51] M. Shirazi, "al-Fiqh series", vols. 107-108, "Economics".

As for the first two categories, the lands are the property of their rightful owners. The land in part 3 belongs to whoever develops it, on the basis of the principle:

"Whoever gives life to a barren land, it is his".[52]

This is so whether this land revitalisation or development is through building, agriculture, river or canal construction, demarcation for the purpose of reasonable forthcoming projects, etc.

No authority has the right to prevent anyone from carrying out such programs or to incur any charges or duties or to demand permission etc. for such tasks.

Article 56

Everyone is free to engage in the building, agriculture, manufacturing industries at any time, and in any form and quality; provided that this does not constitute any harm or the denial of rights to others.[53] The leadership council (of religious scholars) determines the framework for this. Therefore no one may dictate a particular time, quantity or quality and impose them on the one who wants to carry out his activities. Also no one may request any charges, duties etc. for this.

Article 57

Two conditions govern the various forms of business activities and procurement of the permissible:

---

[52] M. Y. al-Koleyni (ed.), "al-Kafi", vol. 3, p 280.

[53] Limitation of Rights:
1. An individual may not cause harm to himself such as suicide, or any other self-inflicting damage.
2. One may not harm or deny the rights of those linked to him, such as his family or those in his care.
3. One may not harm or deny the rights of others such as his/her neighbours by noise nuisance for example, or by building high walls or implantation which deprive their neighbours of, say, sun light, etc. or any other form of harm or interference in their domains or affairs.
4. One may not act against the public interest, for example by not complying with the traffic regulations, or selling foodstuff not suitable for human consumption, etc.
5. One may not engage in acts not covered by the above four categories but are illicit according to Islamic law; such as production and sale of alcohol, wastage of one's foodstuff e.g. burning wheat crops, etc.
M. Shirazi, "al-Fiqh series", 150 vols., vol. 100, "The Rights", pp 324-327.

1. that such activities are not declared illicit by Islam, e.g. trade in alcoholic drinks, gambling.

2. that such activities do not constitute any harm to any individual or group, since *"No (one may) harm (anyone) nor (be) harmed (by anyone) in Islam."* [54]

Article 58

Everyone has the freedom to choose their profession and pursuit and practice their career as they wish, as well as having the freedom to choose whom to work for or with.

Every employer is free to choose the employee he requires.

Every farm owner is free to choose the farm worker he requires and every farm worker is free to choose the farm owner to work for.

Neither of the two parties may pressure the other into anything. The pressure may not take any form, directly or indirectly such as social or psychological pressure. The (employment) contract must be based on agreement (of both parties) with respect to time, wage etc.

Article 59

As mentioned earlier, the Islamic government must meet the needs of the people. The government must support an individual who cannot find employment. An individual who is engaged in a low-paid employment must receive additional support from the government in order to cover all their needs. The government may not force an employer to pay its worker(s) certain wage or limit the hours the worker(s) may work.

The government may intervene if the employer was being unfair or violating the worker(s) right, or if the worker was forced to work for the employer, even through indirect and non-physical pressure such as peer, social or psychological pressure etc.

Article 60

Everyone has the freedom to invest and build up any amount of their wealth and no one may incur any charges or duties on this other than

---

[54] M. H. T. al-Noori (ed.), "Extension for the Guide", vol. 13, p 308.

what has been prescribed by Islam. No one may use their wealth in projects considered illicit.

Article 61

No one has the freedom to invest and build up their wealth through *"usury"*, *"monopoly that has been prohibited in Islam"*[55] and *"trade in the forbidden (products)"*.

Article 62

Everyone has the right to freedom of speech on any issue except illicit aspects such as sacrilegious comments[56], backbiting, slander, etc.

Everyone may debate and criticise government policies, political parties, groups and individuals using the mass media, books, lectures etc.

The framework of such criticisms is the principles of

"To enjoin good and eradicate evil"[57] and *"Advising the Muslim leaders"*

which serve to prevent the greatest danger, which is despotism. No one has the right to deprive those freedoms, whether through prevention, pressure, restrictions or preconditions.

Religious minorities may debate and discuss their beliefs within their own framework.

Article 63

Everyone has the right to freedom of expression, and therefore may write and publish whatever they wish with the exception of those mentioned in Article 62. Everyone is free to establish radio and television broadcasting stations, publishing houses, etc.

---

[55] i.e. those, which involve basic public need such as food and water. Monopolies not prohibited are those such as patent, copyright, etc.

[56] Just as racist remarks are considered to be harmful to the fabric of the society and no racist individuals may air their ideas in public through the mass media, broadcasting sacrilegious views and atheistic beliefs are considered harmful to the society too. However, this does not mean that debates and discussions between monotheists and atheists cannot take place in public or private, etc.

[57] The Qur'an, Repentance (9): 71.

Article 64

Everyone is free to join or establish any organisation, association, union, etc. and organise and attend meetings, rallies, strikes without permissions, duties, etc. The exception is that which is prohibited in Islam according to the recommendation of the elected leadership council of learned scholars.

Article 65

Books, newspapers, magazines, etc. sent through the mail service may not be intercepted or censored. Also telephone calls, telex messages, e-mails, etc. may not be intercepted and monitored. Such practices are considered spying which is forbidden in Islam, *(O ye who believe! avoid suspicion as much (as possible): for suspicion in some cases is a sin: and spy not on each other, nor speak ill of each other...)*[58]

Article 66

The government has no right to search houses or prevent individuals from practising their professions or the means of exercising their rights and using their wealth.

Article 67

Everyone is free to eat and drink what they wish and live where they like. The government may not force an individual out of the place/country of their residence. Similarly it may not force an individual to live in an area against their will. Also everyone is free to choose the type and size of the house to live in and marry whomever he or she want, with the exception of the illegal and illicit practices in all the above issues.

Article 68

Everyone is free to travel at anytime, to any destination and reside at any location for any duration of time. No one may deny him the right to travel and to reside, or restrict his rights in doing so, or charge him for doing so, or force him to seek permission to exercise this right.

---

[58] The Qur'an, The Private Apartments (49): 12.

There exceptions to this, such as children and the married woman as detailed in the jurisprudence texts.[59]

Article 69

Everyone is free to accompany with him or despatch any luggage. Smuggling therefore is not recognised in Islam, and no one may deny this right, or incur charges for this. [60]

Article 70

Everyone is free to seek knowledge in any branch of science, and to educate his/her children in any field. The exceptions to this are:

- the basic teachings of Islam which every Muslim needs to know and practice, and the required expertise which society needs; and

- the seeking of illicit knowledge such as witchcraft which is prohibited.

No one may force anyone to learn and/or teach (any subject), or force anyone to stop learning and/or teaching, except for the mandatory and the illicit. Of course, the government must create the suitable atmosphere for learning and teaching and promote education through incentives and encouragement.

Article 71

Everyone is free to join the armed forces - in the Islamic system of government - and is also free to abstain. The exceptions to this are:

- if the minimum requirements of the armed forces have not been met;

- emergency circumstances such as war, if and when it was necessary for all to participate.

---

[59] Family relationships call for members of the family to co-ordinate their activities and therefore children must seek permission from their parents or guardians and also the married woman from her husband.

[60] The author here is outlining the fundamental right of mankind, provided this exercise does not constitute any harm to the society or any member of the public.

No one may force anyone to join these forces or restrict the time and location for those who have joined.

Article 72

Everyone is free to bury their dead wherever they wish, and to wash and shroud their dead for the burial ceremony as they see fit, without permission and duties.

Article 73

Finally, everyone is free in all her/his actions and practices regarding her/his self, wealth, society, family, and the entire fundamental permissible (acts). The exceptions to this are those actions, which Islam has either required or prohibited. The ratio of these exceptions to the freedoms is insignificant, contrasting man-made laws in the secular system where a vast number of freedoms are suppressed.

Chapter 13: Services

Article 74

The various agencies and departments in a country are divided into three categories:

(A) departments which are entirely necessary,

(B) departments which are entirely unnecessary,

(C) departments which are fundamentally required but partly redundant.

Examples of group (A) are rail, mail, telecommunication, water, electricity services, etc. Such organisations are recognised in Islam and should operate according to the regulations of the Islamic government [61].

The government must allow individuals and (private) companies to establish such organisations. If the turnout for such schemes were not sufficient to meet the demand, the government itself must institute such organisations to provide the services required. The government may exercise its freedom in these aspects provided this does not

---

[61] Islamic government regulations are to secure the right of the individual and prevent monopoly of basic needs in the society.

breach Islamic law (e.g. create unlawful monopolies) or constitute any harm to others.

Examples of organisations in category (B) are: the prison service, custom and excise, travel permission office, immigration and nationality department, visa and residency department, illicit espionage, tax office, burial permission, etc. Such organisations are illegal according Islamic law, since each of those suppresses **countless freedoms and breaches the rights and dignities (of individuals) in addition to the exhaustion of time, wealth and energy.**

Under a true Islamic system of government, all such organisations will be eliminated to relieve the public of their burden and constraints and have their freedoms and dignities returned back to them.

As for those of group (C), an example for this category is a Justice department when one judge rules according to Islamic law and another according to the man-made law. In an Islamic system the practice of the latter judge is not required. Under an Islamic system of government anything that is redundant and superfluous to requirement is eliminated and anything, which is in demand, is fully functional. The redundant services and other bureaucracies are regarded as illegal in Islam since they suppress freedom and waste time, resources and dignities.

The aim of eradicating these services is not to bring about chaos, but the aim of releasing freedoms is the advancement and progress of society and to strengthen the relations and bonds between the leadership and the public and between members of the community.

Chapter 14: The Judicial System

Article 75

The Judge is a male scholar of Islamic laws who must also satisfy other requirements with regards to faith, self-discipline, adolescence, sound mind, legitimate birth and "known to be a committed Muslim".

Article 76

The witness must satisfy such conditions as adolescence, faith - for either case there are exceptions in rare circumstances - sound mind and "known to be a committed Muslim".

As for the minorities, i.e. people of book etc., they are treated according to their own criteria, on the basis of the principle:

"Enjoin on them whatever they have enjoined on themselves".

Article 77

The judge must rule according to Islamic law and may not do so according to any other law, as stated in the Holy Qur'an: *"If any do fail to judge by (the light of) what Allah has revealed, they are (no better than) Unbelievers."* [62]

When presiding over cases between followers of other religions, the judge may rule according to their own laws on the basis of the principle: *"Enjoin on them whatever they have enjoined on themselves".* [63]

Article 78

A judge may not accept any bribe or present[64] or costs, as they are all illegal and if taken must be returned back to the owner. The judge is paid through the public finances.

Article 79

Everyone is equal in front of the judiciary, with no difference between the highest ranking government officer and other members of the community, men or women.

Anyone who is not content with the Islamic judiciary, is not complying with Islamic standard, and the judge must not be deviated by fear or temptation *"And judge thou between them by what Allah has revealed, and follow not their vain desires"*.[65] There must also be provisions to secure the rights of the public.

Article 80

The basis in the case of an accused is innocence and the conviction must be based on evidence.

---

[62] The holy Qur'an, The Table Spread (5): 44.

[63] M. H. al-Hur al-Ameli (ed.), "The Shi'a Guide to Islamic Law", vol. 17, p 485.

[64] which may be regarded as a form of a bribe.

[65] The Qur'an, The Table Spread (5): 49.

The (practice of) defence lawyers in the present days[66] is not recognised by Islam; their practice - in many cases - is illegal and their payments are ill-gotten. Such practices, in many cases, complicate matters further.

Everyone is free to choose a lawyer to represent him, provided that the lawyer believes that the defendant has a case, or that the course of justice depends upon the presence of a lawyer.

Article 81

Everyone has the right to refer to the judicial system without the need of going through the formalities of filling 'in forms, payment of charges and duties, restriction to the use of the jargon of the trade, etc.[67]

Article 82

In Islam there may be different judicial levels within the judicial system, such as district court, court of appeal, supreme court, etc.

Article 83

Islam does not recognise segregation of courts, say, for civil cases and military cases, and their corresponding verdicts, or the segregation of punishments. There is only one law, which applies to all, with one court and one judge.

Chapter 15: Power of the Government and Borders of the Country

Article 84

In principle, the Islamic state does not have borders (between Muslim countries) as we know them today. Everyone is entitled to freedom of

---

[66] i.e. The lawyer uses the system to free the defendant 'on technical grounds' by manipulating the facts in the interest of the accused. As a lawyer, his priority is to win the case for his client rather than to gain justice.

[67] Here the author is stating the fundamental right of the individual and not the procedure. If, say, an individual proves that certain procedure is not correct, he does not loose the right to use the judicial system by not using that procedure.

movement and freedom of trade between two Muslim countries or between Muslim and non-Muslim countries[68].

Article 85

The Islamic government must enable the country to be 'self-sufficient' in science technology, manufacturing, agriculture and every other aspect required.

Article 86

The Islamic government must enable itself to defend the country against any aggression; external or internal:

"Make ready your strength to the utmost of your power."[69]

Article 87

The strength of the government consists of a number of areas; the most important of which is the armed forces. However, recruitment for the armed forces must not be compulsory - according to the Islamic freedom - but voluntary, and the government must encourage the public to join the forces and give incentives to ensure an adequate level of recruitment.

Competition sports in the fields of shooting, racing, etc. may also be used to encourage the public to participate in defence related activities.

Under a true (legitimate) Islamic government, the public must actively take part in the defence of the country if there were the danger of aggression.

Article 88

The security and unity of the entire Islamic State must be totally protected.

---

[68] If entry to a non-Muslim country requires some travel document, then the Islamic government must issue the required travel document to the individuals concerned. Also if the non-Muslim country imposes trade duties, then the Islamic government may negotiate this with the country in question.
M. Shirazi, "al-Fiqh series", 150 vols., vol. 102, "The Islamic Government", pp 31-32.
[69] The Qur'an, The Public Estate (8): 60.

Article 89

The Islamic government must support the oppressed wherever they may be; it must rescue them, their country, wealth and honour from any aggressor. Exceptions to this principle are cases recommended by the leadership council of religious scholars. That is the Islamic government honours any treaty entered into with other states.[70]

Article 90

The University for Islamic sciences which consists of thousands of scholars and students, in co-operation with the entire Muslim community, choose a *Marje'*, a learned religious scholar, for the leadership of the Islamic state.

The elected *Marje' is* the chief of staff of the armed forces. If more than one *Marje' were* elected by the public, then a leadership council of these elected scholars is established, which deals with the affairs of the state by majority vote.

In summary, through this outline it is clear that Islam:

- is more amenable to implementation than any other laws or systems,
- supports freedoms to the utmost extent and relieves restriction and difficulties,
- eradicates poverty in the best way,
- fights ignorance and illiteracy and enforces, promotes and popularises education in all forms,
- provides health care in the best form,
- supports the needy and even the traveller who is in need,
- fights crime to the point of its extinction,
- promotes and popularises ethics, virtue and moral values so that society reaches the highest level of humanity,

---

[70] The precedence for this is the '*Hudaybeyah*' peace agreement between the holy prophet (PBUH) and the pagans of Makkah in 628.

- not only seeks and demands peace but also promotes and popularises it,
- resolves the judicial complexities in a way not found in the text books of present laws and systems,
- provides for the government the strength to safeguard against aggression,
- consolidates stability through its system of government,
- provides the minorities under its system security, tranquillity, assurance and peace of mind,
- provides the best possible opportunities for manufacturing, agriculture, construction and trade.

And finally, it is the only system for mankind, which achieves bliss for this world and the hereafter.

And the request to Allah is to guide everyone to whatever He loves and sanctions.

Glory to thy Lord, the Lord of Honour and Power! (He is free) from what they ascribe (to Him)! And Peace on the Messengers! And Praise to Allah, the Lord and Cherisher of the Worlds. And the Blessings of Allah be on Muhammad and his pure and virtuous progeny.

Concluding Remarks

If by the will of Allah the Almighty, the single universal Islamic government is established, the following the must be considered:

1. Freedoms

2. Taxes

3. Punishments

4. Illegal practices of the pre Islamic-government era

5. All other issues of the pre Islamic-government era

Freedoms

Freedoms must be exercised to the furthest possible extent within the Islamic framework.

Political parties, associations, agriculture, trade, manufacturing, travel, residence, freedom of expression, etc. are all free to an extent not even practised in the west.[71]

This is because the basic principle in Islam is

"The people are in charge of their own self and wealth."

There are a few exceptions such as practices, which are declared illegal in the Qur'an and the Teaching of the Prophet, as well as such regulations introduced by government agencies as traffic regulations.

---

[71] The author discusses these in details in some his books, such as:
- The New Order for the World of Faith, Freedom, Prosperity and Peace
- al-Fiqh, vols. 101-102: "Islamic Government"
- al-Fiqh, vol. 100: "Rights"
- al-Fiqh, vol. 139: "Law"
- al-Fiqh, vols. 105-106: "Politics"
- al-Fiqh, vols. 107-108: "Economics"
- al-Fiqh, vols. 109-110: "Sociology"

On the basis of the same principle, in a similar case to that of followers of other religions (people of the Book), the so called minorities[72] who live in the Islamic state have their freedom, provided they do not disrupt the system regulations such as the traffic regulations and also do not practice illegal acts such as drinking alcohol in public. Furthermore, *they are treated according to their own criteria.*

Taxes

There are no taxes in Islam other than the four mentioned in Article 31. If the government needed further capital, this may be earned from trade and procurement and similar sources.

The government may borrow from the public provided this does not involve usury. (In order to raise a required capital to fund a particular project) the government may enter into a business program, *Mudharabah*[73], with the nation according to the *Mudharabah* regulation.

The land is not for the government to sell but it is *"for Allah and whoever develops it"*. However, the government has the right to procure barren land to an extent that it does not deprive the public from this right and that this (procurement) should be in the interest of the public purse.

As the government - under the Islamic System - grants the widest choice of freedoms to the public, it will not require an army of civil servants and therefore does not have a colossal level of expenditure for unnecessary issues.

---

[72] There is no such term as minority in Islam since it does not recognise this concept. Islam respects mankind to the extent that it seeks to look at those who do not believe in Islam or even in monotheism as equal to the rest. In a document instructing his appointed governor of Egypt; Malek al-Ashtar, Imam Ali (PBUH) states: *". . . as for the people, they are either your brothers in religion or your equal in creation."*

[73] *Mudharabah* is referred to a business investment program where one party provides the capital and the other the business expertise. The parties share the profits and losses of the initiative as defined by the *Mudharabah* regulations.

M. Shirazi, "Islamic Queries", case numbers 2283-2289, pages 518-519.

Punishments

Many learned scholars have indicated that the punishments (*Hadd*) prescribed in the holy Qur'an and the Teaching may not be exercised unless in the presence of al-Imam al-Mahdi (PBUH)[74]. For this and other reasons[75], (e.g. Article 47), these punishments must be postponed for some years, on the basis of

"Punishments are waived by uncertainties"[76] and

"Do no mischief on the earth, after it has been set in order ..."[77]

The *Hadd* punishments may be replaced by other forms of punishments such as imprisonment, fine or deprivation of some of the rights such as driving, etc. This is so that the situation does not lead to anarchy and lawlessness. In all cases such measures should be kept as minimal as possible, since the basic principle in mankind is freedom as well as respect to wealth and rights.

The level of such measures are recommended by the leadership council of religious scholars after consultation with other scholars, experts, party leaders, unions, and others concerned.

It is imperative that the measures and decisions are taken in the common interest of the public, the government and Islam; taking into account the urgency of the "conflicting" issues involved on the basis of the "priority" principle. On such basis the holy prophet of Islam as well as Imam Ali, peace be upon them, did not execute many *Hadd* punishments. We have mentioned many of these cases in the book "The Islamic Government"[78].

---

[74] Al-Imam al-Mahdi is the last of the infallible Imams promised by the Prophet Muhammad (PBUH) to emerge to bring peace and justice to this Earth. Some religious scholars would argue that we would not be able to establish such a perfect Islamic system of government so that the *"Hadd"* may be exercised. During the time of Al-Mahdi, however, this can be done.

[75] M. Shirazi, "al-Fiqh series", 150 vols., vols. 87-88, "Hudood".

[76] ibid.

[77] The Qur'an, The Heights (7): 56.

[78] M. Shirazi, "al-Fiqh series", 150 vols., vol. 102.

Illicit Practices

At the outset, working parties and committees must be established in order to study and plan the course of actions required to eliminate current illicit practices in the best possible way and to prevent and eradicate the causes associated with them.

As an example, there may be hundreds of prostitutes in the country, and a similar number of centres of alcohol sales, as well as the farms, which supply the products for its production, etc.

The prostitutes must be prevented from their practice, and must be supported through the welfare system until they form their families and find honourable jobs.

The alcohol sale outlets must be converted into premises for legal business activities with moral and financial support from the government. Plans must be drawn up to market the products of those farms that supplied the alcohol production industry, etc.

All Other Issues of the Pre Islamic-Government Era

Islam annuls all previous practices[79] as far as the government[80] is concerned. Therefore no one, faithful or otherwise, may be prosecuted for what they may have committed prior to the establishment of the Islamic government, and specially no scholars, wealthy individuals or those who were in power and authority may be killed.

No one's wealth may be confiscated and no courts may be set up to try the members of the previous government, in fact the basic principle which must be followed in such events is:

"Allah has forgiven whatever has past." and

---

[79] This is the principle stated by *Imam Ridha* (PBUH).

[80] This refers to the era in which the Islamic system of government is not established.

"Go! for you are now at liberty."[81]

Furthermore, if, say, a disturbance or rebellion occurred after the establishment of the Islamic state, the principle of peace and non-violence must be pursued in that case and if the government overcame the rebellion and the event was concluded it should be on the basis of forgiveness (i.e. the government should forgive those who were behind the rebellion). The precedent for this is what Imam Ali (PBUH) said in relation to such events about the people of Basra: *"I was gracious to the people of Basra just as the Prophet (PBUH) was to the people of Makkah".*

And the close of our call is: *"Praise be to Allah, the Cherisher and Sustainer of the Worlds!"*

Karbala

Muhammad Shirazi

17.4.1389 H (1969)

---

[81] These are the famous remarks the prophet (PBUH) made when the city of *Makkah* fell to the Muslims and the leaders of *Makkah*, who had gone back on their agreement with the Prophet a year before, were forgiven for what they have done.

39

The Surah (Chapters) of the holy Qur'an referred to in this text

Surah No.	Surah Name
2	The Cow
3	The House of Imran
5	The Table Spread
7	The Heights
8	The Public Estate
9	Repentance
49	The Private Apartments
60	The Tested

Glossary

Ahl-ul-Bayt   "The Household of the prophet". This refers to the Prophet, his daughter Fatimah and the 12 Imams of his progeny.

Ali   Ali is the first of the 12 infallible Imams (leaders) appointed by the Prophet, on Allah's instructions, to succeed him to lead the Muslims.

Allah   Allah is the Arabic name (*Eloh* in Hebrew) for the only creator of all existents.

Anfaal   The extra thing above and beyond the required with regard to a particular aspect. For example the extra prayer offered. Anfaal is also referred to those items that are not owned by anyone such as the peaks of the mountains, villages abandoned by its inhabitants, wealth left behind by a deceased who does not have any inheritors, etc. These belong to Allah and His messenger - that is to say, to the State, to be used for the common weal. The spoils of war are also classified as Anfaal.

Bayt-el-Maal   The Central Bank. May also be referred to as the Treasury.

Emeer-ul-Mu'meneen   *Emeer-ul-Mu'meneen is* the title the Prophet Muhammad, PBUH, exclusively granted to Ali, PBUH, which means Master of the Faithful.

Fiqh   Jurisprudence.

Hadd   The punishment that is specifically defined by the Qur'an or the prophet.

Halaal   Legal, Permissible.

Haraam	Illegal, Illicit, Prohibited.
Imam	Leader. In the specific sense, Imam refers to those 12 successors appointed by the prophet, on Allah's instructions, to lead the Muslims after him. The first of them being Imam Ali and the last of them Imam Mahdi, who has been promised by the prophet to emerge to establish peace and justice throughout the world.
Infallible	A state achieved by an individual, and through Allah's grace, which gives the individual complete freedom from the possibility of being in error. The prophet, his daughter Fatimah and the 12 Imams are infallible.
Islam	Islam is derived from the Arabic word for peace, and it is harmony and submission to the laws of Allah and thus the teachings of Islam are based on the nature of mankind. Islam is a set of teachings that has been revealed by Allah to mankind. The revelation of Islam has taken place, at various times, through different messengers of Allah such as Noah, Abraham, Moses, Jesus and finally Muhammad peace be upon them.
Jizyah	Under the Islamic system of government, Jizyah is the tax that is paid by the non-Muslims living in the Islamic state. The non-Muslims do not pay either the Khums or the Zakat taxes. They are not obliged to join the armed forces to defend the Islamic state whereas the Muslims are. The defence of the non-Muslims' lives, wealth, dignity, etc. is the responsibility of the Islamic state.
Khiraaj	It is the government's income from letting a particular category of land to developers.
Khums	Khums is the tax of 20% levied on untaxed, superfluous annual income. The taxed capital is not subjected to future Khums tax.

Mahdi	Imam Mahdi is the last of the infallible Imams promised by the Prophet Muhammad, PBUH, to emerge to bring peace and justice to this Earth.
Marje'	A Marje' is a Mujtahid who also satisfy other requirements such faith, self-discipline, etc. to be a "mentor" or a "leader".
Mujtahid	A Mujtahid is a learned scholar of Islamic sciences such as Logic, Jurisprudence, Qur'an, Teachings of the prophet, etc. who has the expertise and ability to derive the appropriate rulings for cases in question.
Qur'an	The Qur'an is the holy Book of Islam and it is the transcript of the Divine revelations made to the prophet by Allah. After each revelation, its contents were communicated to the Muslims and precisely recorded.
Sunnah	The Sunnah is the "Words & Deeds" or the Conduct and Teaching of the prophet that serve as guidelines and a source of legislation to Muslims.
Ta'zeer	Any punishment that is not defined in the Qur'an or by the Sunnah but established by the judge.
Zakaat	Zakaat is the tax on nine items when over certain limit. These items are Wheat, Barley, Dates, Raisins, Gold, Silver, Camels, Cows, and Sheep.

References

Seas of Lights	*Behar-ul-Anwar.* The Behar was compiled by the Muslim scholar Muhammad Baqer al-Majlesi into 110 volumes.
The Shi'a Guide to Islamic Law	*Tafseel Wassa'el al-Shi'a ela Tahseel Massa'el al-Shari'a.* Compiled by the Muslim scholar Muhammad Hassan al-Hur al-Ameli
Supplement to the Shi'a Guide	*Mostadrak al-Massa'el* Compiled by the Muslim scholar Mirza Hussain al-Noori
The Suffice	*Al-Kafi* Compiled by the Muslim scholar Muhammad Yaqub al-Koleyni

Each of the above books is a collection of the Teaching of and quotes from the 14 infallible leaders.

M. Shirazi, "al-Fiqh series", 150 vols., vols. 29-32: "Zakat"
M. Shirazi, "al-Fiqh series", 150 vols., vol. 33: "Khums"
M. Shirazi, "al-Fiqh series", 150 vols., vols. 87-88: "Hudood"
M. Shirazi, "al-Fiqh series", 150 vols., vol. 99: "The Rule of Islam"
M. Shirazi, "al-Fiqh series", 150 vols., vols. 105-106: "Politics"
M. Shirazi, "al-Fiqh series", 150 vols., vols. 107-108: "Economics"
M. Shirazi, "al-Fiqh series", 150 vols., vols. 101-102: "Islamic Government"
M. Shirazi, "al-Fiqh series", 150 vols., vol. 138: "Freedoms"
M. Shirazi, "The New Order for the World of Faith, Freedom, Prosperity and Peace".
M. Shirazi, "Islamic Queries".
A. Moir and B. Moir, "Why Men Don't Iron", HarperCollins Publishers, 1998.

Bibliographies

M. Shirazi, "al-Fiqh series", 150 vols., vol. 100: "The Rights"
M. Shirazi, "al-Fiqh series", 150 vols., vol. 139: "Law"